WITHDRAWN

Mexican Architecture
of the Vice-Regal Period

THE author's introduction to Mexico was through the courtesy of EMAN L. BECK and WILLIAM F. BUCKLEY to whom he gratefully acknowledges his indebtedness

Mexican Architecture
of the Vice-Regal Period

BY
WALTER H. KILHAM, S.B., F.A.I.A.

LONGMANS, GREEN AND CO.
55 FIFTH AVENUE, NEW YORK
39 PATERNOSTER ROW, LONDON, E.C.4
TORONTO, BOMBAY, CALCUTTA AND MADRAS
1927

*The author wishes to express his appreciation for the
drawing and photographs contributed by* A. W. K.
BILLINGS, HOWARD FISHER, *and* C. B. WAITE

PRINTED IN THE UNITED STATES OF AMERICA
BY THE PLIMPTON PRESS, NORWOOD, U·S·A

List of Plates

Mexican Architecture
of the Vice-Regal Period

ALTHOUGH Mexico possesses many monuments more worthy of study than some of the models which have been sketched and measured by successive generations of students, relatively very little is known of Mexican architecture in the United States or Europe. In the case of Americans, the supposedly superior attractions of Europe have no doubt hindered the growth of a sympathetic understanding and appreciation of this vast collection of architectural wealth which lies at their very doors.

As a race the Spaniards were the greatest builders since the Romans, and nowhere was this talent displayed to greater advantage than in the royal province of Mexico, or New Spain. The skill, taste, and originality of the Spaniards were supplemented by the high artistic development of the natives, who quickly became as adept as their masters. Even today, love of beauty is a marked characteristic of the descendants of the Aztecs, a quality for which they receive small credit from the more practical Americans and Europeans.

The history of architecture in Mexico during the period under consideration represents a complete cycle, beginning with the direct importation of the Middle Renaissance style from Spain, where Juan de Herrera, the architect of the Escorial, the Cathedral of Valladolid, and other well-proportioned but highly formal buildings, represented the dominant note in ecclesiastical architecture, and gave the name of *herreriana* to the productions of his school. In the old country the Renaissance progressed through the Plateresque, Churrigueresque, and Baroque manners, to arrive again at the end of the eighteenth century at the formalities of a style which corresponded closely to the Empire style in France. In New Spain architectural design swung farther away, along a path influenced by native ideas as well as Spanish fashions, through a dazzling climax of half-Indian, half-Spanish extravaganza, finally to reach the same goal, the elegant and formal *Academismo,* which completed the most remarkable excursion in architectural design known to the history of the Renaissance.

There is, naturally, no Gothic in Mexico, but in the Renaissance way the country's splendid churches, sweetly domed and nobly towered, and its massive and time-stained palaces, are products of a really great architecture, well-conceived, thoroughly understood, and marvellously well-executed.

Building activity started in 1521, immediately after the Conquest, and lasted until the beginning of the disturbances which terminated in the independence of Mexico in 1821. The province enjoyed a period of unexampled prosperity, free from war or civil dissension of any kind, for nearly three centuries, which may be designated as the Vice-Regal period, during which its wealth increased to an astonishing extent.

In addition to its skill in architecture and building,

the ruling class had the assistance of a plentiful supply of cheap but intelligent labor, for the native Indians, many of whom were already skilled artisans, learned all sorts of crafts with surprising facility and were remarkably amenable to supervision. The union between the government of the colony and the ecclesiastical authority, however doubtful as a practical measure, was a powerful stimulus to the cause of architecture, and large building projects were carried out in every direction. In fact, according to a Mexican writer, so ardent in the cause of religion were the followers of Cortés and Pizarro that in the same breath they informed the Indians of their new Sovereigns, the Emperor Don Carlos and the Creator, the two allegiances being inseparable.

So rapid was the development of building after the country had been pacified, that by 1596, only seventy-five years after the Conquest, over four hundred monasteries had been built, in addition to the civil and domestic buildings, and churches, of which latter there were over a thousand in one province alone. As the population and wealth of the Colony increased, so numerous did the churches become that no village hacienda or ranch could be found, no matter how small, without its chapel. For example, one writer says that, after travelling on horseback for days in apparently virgin territory and crossing almost impassable districts where seemingly no one had been before, one would find at the journey's end a handsome, even sumptuous edifice as evidence of the faith, energy, and incomparable labor of the Church during the seventeenth and eighteenth centuries. Built and often

vaulted with stone, these churches, as well as the dwell-
ings, were at first of a rather fortress-like severity in
style, due to lack of resources and the wish to obtain se-
curity in a country only recently subdued. As tranquil-
lity and prosperity increased, both religious and private
buildings gradually developed a style of exceeding richness and elaboration, which culminated in such buildings as the Parroquias of Taxco and Tepozatlán, and
the palace of the Conde del Valle de Orizaba in Mexico
City.

Unlike the practice of Rome, which allowed and
encouraged her dependencies such as Egypt, Judea,
Greece, etc., to continue their own language, religion,
and architecture, or of England, which allows her Indian subjects, for example, full liberty of creed and
culture, the Spanish colonists by force of arms up-
rooted and destroyed as far as possible all traces of
Aztec civilization, laws, religion, and social atmosphere, replacing them fully and completely with their
own. Especial care was taken by Cortés, *el conquis-
tador del Anáhuac*, in sketching the plan of the new
Capital which was to rise on the ruins of Tenoxtitlán,
to locate the new temple at the north side of the great
square, lately occupied by the *teocalli* of the bloody
Huitzilopochtli, while the site of the former palace of
Moctezuma was assigned to the seat of the new government. This policy was carried out likewise in other
places, and where, as in the case of the pyramid of
Cholula, the original *teocalli* was too large to remove,
a Christian temple was erected on its summit, a zeal
in the cause of religion which later came to be re-
gretted.

The development of the Colonial style in Mexico is comparatively simple. Although, with characteristic Spanish independence, Juan Gil de Hontañon was at the time of the Conquest building in Spain the cathedrals of Salamanca and Segovia in the pointed style, the Gothic period had passed, leaving only reminiscences which in Mexico were expressed in the rib vaulting of one or two early buildings. In one church, the Capilla Real at Cholula, built as an " overflow " for the adjoining San Gabriel, the guiding influence was quite evidently the mosque of Cordoba with its many aisles and interior columns.

During the earliest years of the Colony's history the disorders peculiar to an only recently conquered and scarcely yet pacified country, where the fear of insurrection was mingled with quarrels and struggles among the Conquerors, were responsible for the severe and fortress-like character of the early buildings. The churches were characterized by thick walls, and massive buttresses with low and squat towers. Domestic buildings were one story high and often provided with *almenas* (battlements), while the still scanty resources of the settlements prevented any great use of ornament. The fine basilica-like church of Coyoacan, and the cathedral and chapel of the Tercer Orden at Cuernavaca, illustrate the ecclesiastical side of this earlier style, while the houses of Alvarado and Cortés at Coyoacan, dating from 1523, are good types of the domestic architecture of the primitive period.

In Spain at the middle of the sixteenth century the architects Juan de Herrara, Juan de Toledo, and Juan Gomez de Mora represented the growing taste for the severely classical school which, employing only the Doric order and avoiding ornament, gave to its works an indubitable aspect of strength and power. This school which, as was said above, came to be known as *herreriana,* and whose most important Spanish building was the Escorial, strongly influenced the first part of the Colony's career. The great cathedrals of Mexico City and Puebla are the most splendid examples of the style in New Spain.

In the buildings of this period the walls are thick, and free from ornament except around the portals where a Doric order, usually of great purity, is employed and is often surmounted by a secondary and smaller simple architectural frame which encloses a niche with a statue of the Saint, and is flanked on each side with pyramidal, or obelisk-like, adornments. The cornices of these buildings are invariably straight, the pediments unbroken, vaults semi-circular, and domes hemispherical, low, and ordinarily octagonal, in plan. There is little intimation in this earlier work of the gorgeous façades and interiors which were to mark the later years of the Colony's prosperity. Barroso well says that " the road which architecture in New Spain followed through different styles and influences, excepting the academic reaction of the nineteenth Century, can be expressed by saying that it was a slow change from inexpressive lines and surfaces to lines and surfaces having the fullest amount of expression." [1]

The Cathedral of Mexico City is probably the largest church in America, (387 feet long and 177 feet wide),

[1] Francisco Diez Barroso, *El Arte en Nueva España.*

and, all in all, perhaps the finest. Its rather low and heavily buttressed façade and majestic towers seem to express the very essence of Latin American spirit. The church deserves to be better known; I question if a more satisfying Renaissance cathedral exists in the world.

The original design, laid out by Castañeda, was supplemented after the corner stone had been laid, in 1573, by a new project, the work of Juan Gomez de Mora, who was sent from Spain by Philip III. The plan has some points in common with the cathedrals of Salamanca and Segovia, though it lacks the apsidal chapels.

While the severity of the Doric treatment of the interior may detract from its interest, its great size and height (179 feet in the dome), and its complete unity of design, make it sufficiently impressive, and the vista through the archway into the adjoining Sagrario Metropolitano, with its play of light and shade punctuated by the moving figures of black-clad worshippers, is exceedingly picturesque. The detail of its two great towers is well worthy of careful study, while their similarity in several respects to the towers of the Escorial is an interesting evidence of their Spanish ancestry.

The plans for the Cathedral of Puebla were approved by Philip III in 1562, although the building was not finished until 1649. It is smaller than the Cathedral of Mexico, and of greater homogeneity, but its exterior is somehow less interesting, although its lines and details are of much elegance. The interior greatly resembles the Cathedral of Mexico, except that the altars, *rejas* and carvings seem richer. The architect was probably Mora, though some authorities ascribe it to Herrara. The view of the building from across the Alameda at the rear will be found the most pleasing.

Another great church of the earlier period before native influence was strongly felt is San Augustín Acolman, whose tasteful friezes, carved with fruits and garlands, might almost claim a place in Toledo or Salamanca.

The great *tezontle* palaces in Mexico City, of which the Casa del Conde de Santiago de Calimaya is an instance, sometimes called the Palace of Santiago, exemplify the domestic architecture of the time. Two great stories in height, the dominant note is that of severity and force. Even the stone gargoyles are carved in the form of cannon, and the battlements were surmounted by a row of stone soldiers until a republican government ordered their removal.[2]

In these palaces, which presented few windows to the street, the life of the family and retainers went on under the lofty arcades of the great patio. The family apartments and the chapel were in the upper story, away from the dampness of the ground and open to the breezes. If the house was in the plateau country the roof was flat, supported by great wooden beams, and paved with flat red bricks laid in lime on a bed of dry earth which formed a perfect insulation from the heat and cold, and, marvelous to relate, was water-

[2] A decree of the Government of May 2, 1826, ordered the destruction of coats-of-arms and other insignia which recorded the dependence of Mexico upon Spain. A prominent exception was the equestrian statue of Charles IV of Spain, on whose pedestal the words were added " Mexico preserves it as a monument of art."

tight. At lower elevations, in the warmer and moister zones, sloping, tiled roofs provided shelter against the greater rainfall. The ornament of the façade was generally concentrated around the portals or occasionally at the corner, but often, as in the case of the house of the Mayorazgo de Guerrero, or the house in the Calle de Relox, the niche which surmounted the corner was elaborately decorated and formed the principal ornament of the façade.

As the wealth and prosperity of the Colony increased it found ample expression in the character of the multitudes of new buildings which sprang up in every direction. The progress of the successive Renaissance periods in Spain was reflected in Mexican work, which often surpassed that of the mother country in elaboration, but absolutely without servile imitation; so that it should be studied by itself without any attempt to associate it with the Spanish.

The natural resources of the country, together with its remarkable activity in agriculture, mining and commerce, and its long freedom from disturbance under a stable and not illiberal government, caused a remarkable prosperity which brought unheard-of luxury within reach of the rich, and reasonable ease and comfort to the poor. Hospitals and colleges multiplied, as well as churches and palaces. The University came into being by royal order as early as 1553. Other institutions followed, such as the Academia de Belles Artes, the Monte de Piedad, and the great Colegio de las Vizcainas whose enormous façades, nearly 500 feet in length, are among the most striking in the capital. Other foundations during the eighteenth century were the Hospital des Terceros, the Casa de Cuna, the Hospicio de Pobres, and the Hospital de San Andrés, which institutions alone comprised a complete plan of benefices for the Capital. The Viceroys were frequently able men, active in advancing the welfare of New Spain. Some, like Mendoza, the Velascos, Bucareli, and Revillagigedo, were of rather exceptional brilliancy. Aqueducts were built, streets paved and lighted, and banditry suppressed. The English traveler, Thomas Gage, speaking of the life of the Colony in 1624–25, stated that there were four things to see in New Spain; the women, the clothes, the horses, and the streets, and says he should have added a fifth, the trains of the nobility, which were far more splendid than those of the court of Madrid or of any capital of Europe. The geographer Humboldt later was so impressed that he called the capital the " City of Palaces," and even today, in spite of the growth of cities in the United States, it is perhaps, all told, the handsomest city in North America, with the possible exception of Washington.

During this period the government required works of public utility, such as aqueducts, canals, roads, bridges and forts; private individuals built spacious and richly decorated houses and palaces, with elaborately designed portals and patios, while the furnishings were of mahogany, ebony and rosewood, often richly inlaid with silver and pearl. Silks from China, and brocades and velvets from Spain, were common decorations. The clergy established large, rich and dazzling temples, adorned with gold, and hung with pictures by the rising school of Mexican painters whose productions still hold the admiration of sophisticated visitors.

Under these influences the way was open for the importation and surprising development of the more highly ornamented and costly Plateresque and Barroco styles, which were at their height in the mother country. Beginning with gradual softening of the rigid lines of the *herreriana,* the severe Doric of the church portals changed to twisted and garlanded Corinthian; rectangular windows became octagonal or star-shaped; straight entablatures and cornices developed curves and convolutions, while decorative patterns covered the surfaces of panels, columns and borders. The work of the Plateresque period may be studied in the Convent of La Merced in Mexico City as well as in the beautiful San Augustín, now the National Library, whose proportions and details are of remarkable elegance, while in domestic architecture the houses of the Conde del Valle de Orizaba and San Mateo Valparaiso illustrate the diversity of the style and the versatility of the architects of the period.

Illustrations of the Barroco are so numerous that only a few can be cited. The Capilla del Pocito at Guadalupe Hidalgo, the domes of El Carmen at San Angel, the "House of the Masks" and "Las Vizcainas," may be noted as a few prominent examples, but so varying are the Mudejar, Indian, and Spanish influences which affected their design that a chronological classification according to style would be very difficult. The capricious forms of windows, balconies, and niches, and the brilliant profiling of the mouldings whose faces are ingeniously pitched to catch and reflect high lights, well express the growing taste for luxury and ostentation in the now powerful colony, which reached its climax in the Churriguer-esque of the latter part of the eighteenth century, when ordinarily simple architectural forms assumed shapes of hitherto unimagined elaboration and expressive-ness.

In the churches of El Sagrario and La Santísima in Mexico City, designed in 1749 and 1755 respectively, the architect, Lorenzo Rodríguez, certainly produced two temples of notable originality and beauty. The pink *tezontle* façades of the former, which frame and enclose the gray masses of detail around and above the portals, form, with the adjoining cathedral, a most re-markable composition whose striking mass and out-line are in no way impaired by the riotous intricacy of the detail.

The introduction of glazed faience was followed by its use for the decorations of domes, towers and walls, and its brilliant coloring seen against the intense blue of the sky, added another note to the already dazzling scheme. The surprising fact is that throughout all this riot of elaborate decoration and color, the innate Span-ish good sense always retained ample surfaces of plain masonry as a background and frame for the ornament, even in the most extravagant buildings, and the parti-colored domes invariably rose above a base of severely plain stone, so that the effect of the whole was never confused. In this respect alone, Mexican architecture is worthy of the most careful study. Even such struc-tures as the " House of Tiles " in Mexico City, or the

Casa del Alfeñique at Puebla, which are among the most beautiful buildings in the world, show a balance of elaboration which could only have been conceived in an atmosphere of architectural sanity.

In the last years of the eighteenth century the world-wide classical reaction brought about the cold and formal *Academismo*, of which the leading exponent was Manuel Tolsa, a young Valencian sculptor, who arrived from Spain in 1791, commissioned as Director of Sculpture in the Academia of San Carlos. This title, in passing, may raise in the reader's mind a slight speculation as to the status or condition of the art schools in the United States at that period. In Mexico City the Academy had been a going concern since 1783, and had exerted a definite influence on the art of the Capital. At any rate, the new Director soon gave evidence of extensive knowledge and good taste in the field of architecture as well as sculpture, and in 1797 he was entrusted with the design of the vast new Royal School of Mines, or the " Mineria," which is the principal example of the Academic style in the Capital. This correct and cold design comprises long exterior façades, which are now much disfigured by excessive settlement of the foundations, and a majestic interior court of 645 square meters, with a grand staircase which challenges comparison with the best work in the mother country. Tolsa also designed the palace of the Condesa de Pérez Gálvez, in the Calle del Puente de Alvarado, and the church of Nuestra Señora de Loreto, whose exterior, more reserved and correct than attractive, is surpassed by the interior rotunda, which, although raised on a hexagonal plan, has fine proportions and much merit. This church also suffers from the treacherous subsoil and leans badly, so that Tolsa is probably best remembered by his work on the façade and central lantern of the Cathedral of Mexico, and by his truly splendid bronze of Charles IV, in the Avenida Juarez, which easily takes place among the world's best equestrian statues. This was cast in one piece in Mexico City in 1802, another side light on the advanced condition of the arts in Mexico at that period.[3] So preponderating was Tolsa's personality that many of the important works of his time have come to be attributed to him instead of to their rightful authors, and this tendency extends even to the furniture and silverware of the academic period.

Francisco Eduardo Tresguerras, a picturesque native of Celaya, deserves mention at this point. Like a true artist of the Renaissance he was not only a painter of merit and painted the decorations for his own churches, but attained a certain fame as a writer of sonnets. His style was softer and more graceful than Tolsa's and his masterpiece, El Carmen of Celaya, deserves to be more widely known. Some incidents of the life of Tresguerras, as related by Terreros[4] are interesting, and the picture of his declining years must excite a feeling of envy among the architects of these hurried years. Although most of his life was spent in the small city of Celaya, it contained several striking incidents. He held the offices of *sindico, regidor,* and *alcalde,* of his native city. He took part in the unsuc-

---

[3] Lorado Taft in his *American Sculpture* states that the first casting of an equestrian statue in the United States was Clark Mills' "General Jackson," in Washington, which was erected in 1853.

[4] D. Manuel Romero de Terreros, *Arte Colonial.*

cessful insurrection against the Spanish government headed by the patriot Hidalgo, but escaped punishment when it was suppressed. Nobody could deny that he had the soul of an artist. In the last years of his life, every afternoon he would go on foot to a little haçienda of his, called " El Romerillo," in the environs of Celaya. With his great cape over his shoulders he would march along, playing his flute and followed by his faithful and inseparable dog. Then he would sit down under a tree, and with all the simplicity of a child alternate between playing with his dog and calling forth the notes of his favorite instrument. From this improvised Arcadia he could enjoy the peaceful landscape, and contemplate with the highest satisfaction the distant outlines of the greatest works of his active life. Not until the herds came slowly down to the waters of the Laja and the last rays of the sun illumined the lovely dome of Carmen, would he retrace his steps to his home in the city.

The history of Mexican architecture as such terminated with the *Academismo*. Since the independence, design, much of which is highly meritorious, has followed European models, mostly French, with few local characteristics. At present there is some indication of a new school of Mexican thought whose inspiration is based on the splendid native art tradition of the Aztecs and Mayas, and in this the future hope of Mexican design may lie.

While the foregoing represents the main trend of Mexican Colonial architecture, it was at the same time deeply affected by several important local influences.

In Spain much of the Gothic and all the later work shows the presence of the Mudejar influence, or that of the Christianized Moors, and it is natural that this quality of Spanish work should have gone overseas along with the rest. Among the earlier buildings of the Capital many good examples remain of over-all stucco wall patterns of geometric figures, which plainly show a Moorish ancestry. These stucco patterns had attained considerable elaboration when the increase of resources brought about the general use of the more expensive and showy Puebla tile, or else genuine cut stone for wall surfaces, in the carving of which there became evident a new spirit. Friezes and garlands intended as pure Renaissance took on unexpected shapes and lines, while spiral terminations of friezes and belts likewise showed the hand of the Aztec workman, involuntarily recording on the walls of his master's house the pathetic tradition of his lost race. Necessarily much of the builder's work was done by Indian mechanics, and probably architects as well, who would, of course, follow their natural bent in executing their work. This overtone of Aztec design is one of the most charming and original qualities which runs through all Mexican architecture, and gives it a strong individuality of its own, apart from European precedent.

The religious influence also had a deep effect upon domestic architecture as attested by the *nichos*, carved high up on street corners and flat walls, and the sacred monograms, which sometimes appeared in cornices and ornaments. No large house was without a fine private chapel which was treated with special magnificence and given the place of honor. Shrines abound

along the roads, and often public works, such as fountains and bridges, are decorated with them.

Some time after the Conquest, in 1526 according to
a popular belief, some potters from Talavera and other
places in Spain came to settle in Puebla and began the
manufacture of the glazed tiles and majolica ware,
which soon came to be utilized for a thousand architectural purposes as well as for household utensils and
vases. Domes and towers soon shone with brilliant
blue, white and yellow; dadoes and stairs, lavabos,
nichos, and even bathtubs in faience were found everywhere. Walls of buildings were covered with it, and, as
in Spain, tile work became an important feature of the
native style, a fact too little recognized by American
imitators.

The story of Mexican tin-enameled faience is a fascinating history in itself. It is believed that the early
friars were impressed by the ability which the natives
showed in the manufacture of earthenware, and sent to
Spain for artisans skilled in pottery-making to come to
the new colony and instruct the natives in the art.
Whatever the source, progress was rapid and the productions of tin-enameled pottery made by the Pueblan
workmen, which came to be known as Talavera ware,
were wide-spread, and their vases, bowls, and other
utensils are now highly prized. From modest begin-
nings the industry developed until, in 1750, some thirty
establishments in the city of Puebla were engaged
in its manufacture.[5] A considerable proportion of the
Pueblan work seems to bear the impress of Chinese de-

[5] Edwin Atlee Barber, *The Maiolica of Mexico.*

sign, which has given rise to the idea that Chinese workmen were brought to Mexico to aid in the production of this ware. Mr. Barber, however, states that this theory is incorrect, and that the pseudo-Chinese decoration is from the hands of local decorators who attempted to imitate the Chinese manner. The nineteenth century saw its decline, but efforts to revive it are on foot. The characteristics of its design ran through the Moresque, Spanish, Chinese, and Hispano-Mexican periods, and the skill of the Mexican potters produced many articles of great beauty and value for which the country has received little credit.

The native Puebla tiles are four and a half to five inches square, generally slightly convex and beveled on the edges, and showing three rough spots in the form of a pea on the upper side, which are the scars left by the clay supports used in baking. The dark blue color is always in relief, due to the thickness of the pigment. The glazing is imperfect, giving a pleasing texture, and the whites are of a greyish tinge.

The buildings in which glazed tiles were used for decoration are legion, and only a few can be named here. In Puebla the churches of Guadalupe, Nuestra Señora de la Luz, San Francisco, and others, will repay examination. Near Mexico City the domes of the Convent of El Carmen at San Angel, together with interior dadoes, lavabos, etc., and the Convent at Churubusco with the little chapel of San Antonio Abad include some fine examples, while in the Capital itself are found innumerable domes and towers, wall panels, and interior work of all sorts. An old house in San Cosme contains a bathroom, complete with walls and

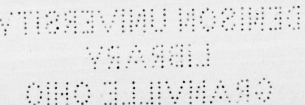

floor all done in tiles, and a large bathtub, the bottom of which displays a life-size depiction of a lady of considerable personal charm.

The use of glazed tiles for exterior decoration persisted up to the end of the Spanish domination. It constituted one of the most engaging phases of Mexican architecture.

But after all matters of detail have been taken into consideration, the distinguishing fact remains that the one dominant feature of Mexican Colonial architecture is the dome, which was universally utilized and of which literally thousands exist, all built of solid masonry. Placed over the crossing of nave and transept churches, or roofing the innumerable chapels and shrines, its use imparts a singular sweetness and beauty to the skyline of the cities, almost unique in the world. The outlines range from a somewhat flattened shape raised on a drum, through the regular half orange to the elongated, almost Persian type of El Carmen at Celaya, and the Chapel of the Well at Guadalupe. The patterns of the colored glazed tiles with which they are covered vary from plain geometrical squares, or zigzags, to the elaborate coats of arms and garlands at San Angel, while the surmounting lanterns are sometimes entirely made of faience instead of stone. They are generally composed of a single shell and almost always are furnished with windows, either in the drum or in the shell itself, so as to admit considerable light to the interior. There is no limit to the number allowed to a church; three, five or seven are common. One church has forty-nine.

The minor accessories of artistic life carried out the effect of the architecture. Furniture, silver and iron work and candlesticks, the wooden doors to the houses and churches, the carved and inlaid *sillerias* of the choirs, and the gorgeous gilded retablos above the altars, all form part of a complete and harmonious whole. In the geometric design of door panelling the reminiscence of Mudejar work is particularly apparent.

The elaborate gilded retablos deserve a monograph. While it is true that many of them are merely banal combinations of tortured friezes, inverted pyramidal pilasters, and corkscrew columns, some, like that of La Ensenañza in Mexico City, for example, are extremely beautiful, while others are not only tasteful, but are marvelous examples of the carver and decorator's work. Often charming medallion-like religious paintings are worked into the decorative scheme, adding greatly to the beauty of the whole.

A word should be added about the early Mexican School of painting, an art here as elsewhere closely allied to architecture, and which in Mexico followed much the same path which led through an early period of works by artists who came over from Spain bringing the Spanish tradition along with them, through a second period of transition when local influences became stronger, and a third period, almost strictly Mexican, which faded into a decadence in the early nineteenth century. During practically all of this time, at least up to the last period, the demand was for paintings of a religious nature, usually subjects from the New Testament, destined for the decoration of the walls of churches and convents, or actually as objects of devotion; mythological or historical subjects were very rare, and the effort was to convey an idea rather than any visual emotion. Notwithstanding this limitation the productions of some of these artists were of remarkable merit, and have frequently excited the admiration of experts.

Among the great names of the first period are those of Echave *El Viejo*, Sebastián de Arteaga, whose work was sometimes mistaken for that of Zurbarán, Luis and José Juárez, Echave *El Mozo*, son of *El Viejo*, Juan Correa, and Cristóbal Villalpando.

Juan Rodríguez Juárez and Nicolas Rodríguez Juárez may be taken to represent the transition, while the great figures of the third period are Miguel Cabrera (1695–1768), a Zapotec Indian, and José Maria Ibarra, called the Murillo of New Spain. Barroso says of Cabrera that not only was his production immense but he was the most famous and sought-for painter in the colony during the second half of the eighteenth century. The demand for his pictures was enormous. Like Rubens he had a large atelier and many assistants, and he introduced a broad and spacious mode of treatment which had an important effect on contemporary Mexican art.

Ibarra (1688–1756) was a brilliant colorist, and he was able to enhance his early reputation as a copyist by developing an originality and coloring which placed him in the same rank with Cabrera.

Francisco Eduardo Tresguerras, of Celaya who has been mentioned as an architect, was also a painter, an etcher, a musician and a poet. His decorations are dramatic and colorful, and he had the satisfaction of placing some of them upon the walls of one of his own creations, El Carmen at Celaya.

The sculpture of the period was evidenced by many reliefs and figures in the *portadas* of the churches, notably the central panel of the front of San Augustín, now the National Library, and by much decorative architectural carving, but on the whole one cannot say that sculpture in its true sense existed prior to Tolsa's arrival. He alone, according to Revilla, was compensation enough for the previous deprivation,[6] for in him the genius of the art made up for all the lost time. Tolsa did not make a great number of statues, as his architectural activities robbed him of the time he might have devoted to sculpture, but the works he did execute all testify to his knowledge, talents, and courage. In addition to his Charles IV, his principal statues were those of the clock on the Cathedral of Mexico, and the Tabernacle of the Cathedral of Puebla.

Aside from the special sculptural works mentioned, it must be said that the architectural carving and plastic decoration of the buildings are much more local in feeling than the painting, and show far less imported influence.

In fact, architects can find an endless mine of suggestion in Mexican domestic architecture and its accessories. A proper consideration of the treatment of balconies, stairways, cornices, and windows, alone would fill a book. A monograph could be made of the

[6] Lic. D. Manuel G. Revilla; *El Arte in Mexico en la Época Antigua y durante el Gobierno Virreinal.*

nichos. A Mexican town house of the older type is approached from the street by great iron-studded doors and a cavernous *zaguan,* reminiscent of Toledo or Segovia, which led to the *patio.* The lower portions of the house are devoted to service, storage, and habitation of a sort for the porter, and maybe several turkeys. Under the arcades, which once sheltered the family coach, Felipe or Vicente will perhaps be found washing the car. A stone stairway swings nonchalantly up to the balcony which is gay with flowers, vines, red peppers, and colored rugs. Brilliantly colored birds in wooden cages hanging from the roof add to the life of the scene. From the balconies, open lofty, possibly rather bare chambers, running through to the street. If the house is in the plateau country another stair leads to the brick paved *azotea* or roof. In the country the house is likely to be even more picturesque and the flowers more profuse.

Gardens, fountains, tiled pools, seats, and well curbs, occur in plenty. Color is everywhere, in the soft weathered pinks, blues and greens of the walls, the gaily enameled domes and towers, the clothing of the native Indians, and the parti-colored fruits and flowers exposed for sale along the streets.

The gentle traffic of patient donkeys and sandal-footed Indians flows noiselessly along the cobbled country roads and down the cool colonnades of the cities. Above the time-stained garden walls rise straight, dark cypresses and rustling eucalyptus. The domes and towers of the village church, massive and eternal, look down into courts gay with roses and bougainvillea, watered by plashing fountains and soothed by the gurgle of covered streams. Across the maize comes the soft chime of distant vespers.

Pink and orange walls, grated windows, palms and cactus, *peones* and *pulque*, snowy volcanoes against an ultramarine sky.

"Where the laden burros patter down the steep and rocky ways,
And Cholula's silver vespers echo sweet across the maize,
Or the holy shrine of Mary guards the magic, mystic well,
And the nopal and the cypress weave their drowsy, dreamy spell,
There's a town along a hillside, basking in the southern haze,
Just below the Tres Marias, where I'd like to end my days.
Houses low, and pink and ancient, thick with purple bloom o'erhung,
Windows barred with antique gratings, same as when old Spain was
young."

PLATE I

Stairway, Santiago Palace

THE Palace of the Count of Santiago de Calimaya, one of the oldest and most magnificent houses in Mexico City, was built soon after the Conquest by a relative of Hernan Cortés, Lic. Don Juan Gutiérrez Altamarino. The exterior walls enclose two large courts, one for the family and one for service. The main court is surrounded by a two-story stone arcade, the loggias of which give access to the various rooms. At the right hand end is placed a splendid carved fountain; at the left the main staircase, built of stone, with an ancient, hand-wrought iron rail, and guarded at the foot by two rather primitive stone dogs, swings up to the main floor level in the nonchalantly superior manner characteristic of Spanish work. Even in the early half of the sixteenth century Mexico possessed stone cutters and masons able to cope with the difficult construction problem of such a stairway as this.

The virile and yet beautiful proportions of the columns and the characteristic mouldings of the arch are worthy of the best Vice-Regal work.

A century after its construction the house became the property of Don Santiago de Calimaya; and it was he who caused a park to be laid out in the neighborhood, and the street along the south side of the house was long known as the Calle del Parque del Conde.

During the Colonial period the house had considerable importance as it was a sort of meeting place for
the aristocracy, and the Viceroy, the Archbishop, and
other dignitaries used to watch religious and civic
parades from its windows as well as the displays of fire-
works which were provided on festival occasions.

I. Stairway, Santiago Palace

PLATE 2

Loggias, Santiago Palace

THE loggias of the main patio are in two stories, and consist of elliptical arches supported on ranges of Doric pillars. The spandrels of the lower range are decorated with armorial bearings carved in stone, while the upper spandrels and cornice are punctuated by heads supporting military-looking stone gargoyles, through which the roof water escapes to the court.

Iron railings, carrying supports for flower pots, fill the spaces between the pillars.

PLATE 3

View in Upper Loggia, Santiago Palace

THE opening at the top of the stairs is covered by a triple-cusped arch elaborately ornamented, a *tour-de-force* which evidently interested the builders even at that early day, while the detail of the side pilasters and border ornament seems to be influenced by Aztec motives rather than Spanish. In the corner of the loggia at the end, beside the painted coat-of-arms, are seen the carved pilasters of the elaborate doorway leading to the family chapel, which occupies the place of honor.

3. View in Upper Loggia, Santiago Palace

2. Loggias, Santiago Palace

PLATE 4

Entrance, Santiago Palace

THIS picture shows the composition of the main entrance, with coupled and fluted columns below and a cusped window above, surrounded by an interlacing filigree border. The door lintel, attractively curved and broken, and the moving figure by the door give an idea of the scale. The famous cannon gargoyles are also visible, and the central space from which the family arms were removed. Statues originally occupied the pedestals over the gargoyles.

PLATE 5

Entrance, House of Don Juan Manuel

MEXICO CITY abounds in legends of every sort, as well as in the old mansions, of which this has one of the best of the minor doorways. The legend pertaining to this particular house, as related by Thomas A. Janvier, has an intriguing beginning:

" This Don Juan Manuel, Señor, was a very rich and worthy gentleman who had the bad vice of killing people. Every night at eleven o'clock, he went out from his magnificent house — as you know, Señor, it is still standing in the street named after him — all muffled in his cloak, and under it his dagger in his hand."

The rest of this narrative is told in the *Legends of the City of Mexico.*

The patio of the house is worthy of its history, but is too narrow to obtain a good photograph.

4. Entrance, Santiago Palace

5. Entrance, House of Don Juan Manuel

PLATE 6

Patio, Santiago Palace

THIS plate shows to still better advantage the construction of the arched stairway at the upper landing, and the detail of the primitive wrought iron railing and braces. The large balls at the corner posts are typical of Mexican work, and the square applications at the centers of the balusters, as well as the ornament at the centers of the braces, are evidently derived from Spanish precedent.

The carved fountain at the other end of the stone-paved patio can be seen under the arcade.

Visitors to the house, are particularly attracted by the curious stone gargoyles on the exterior, carved in the form of cannon (a privilege allowed only to those who held the rank of Capitán-General), and by the head of an Aztec idol which forms the corner stone and is said to have been placed there by the hands of Hernando Cortés himself.

6. Patio, Santiago Palace

PLATE 7

Ancient Balustrade,
Santiago Palace

A DETAIL of the old wrought-iron balustrade, shown
in Plate 1.

PLATE 8

A Gateway in Blue and White

LEADING to the service court of the Santiago Palace.
The decoration and border at the top is in blue Puebla
tile. The vast size of these service courts, now rented
out in shops and swarming with peons, is an indication
of the wealth and power of the original owners.

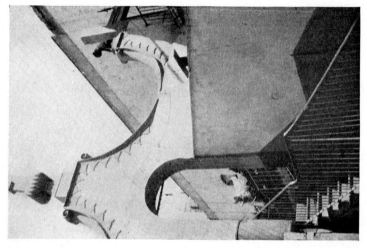

8. A Gateway in Blue and White

7. Ancient Balustrade, Santiago Palace

PLATE 9

The House of Alvarado at Coyoacan

IN the years immediately following the Conquest, perhaps about 1522–1523, the conqueror, Hernando Cortés, and his trusted lieutenant, Pedro de Alvarado, attracted perhaps by the pleasant scenery, the springs, and rippling streams of Coyoacan, built residences here, both of which are now in existence.

The House of Alvarado still possesses its ancient stone-flagged patio, extensive garden watered by diminutive tile and stone aqueducts, embowered in roses and bougainvillea, and massive low walls. The façade is possibly somewhat altered; the shrine and figurine over the door appear to be of later date; but the stucco pattern of the walls must date from some early period, if not the original one. A roof shelter has been added to the *azotea*, or flat tiled roof, of the original house.

The house, now the property of Mrs. Zelia Nuttall, stands not far from the Convent of Churubusco, and faces on a highway which has witnessed many historic events.

PLATE 10

A Doorway, Mexico City

THIS is a fine example of the *herreriana* type of
doorway; a well-proportioned arch framed in a correct Doric combination of fluted pilasters and simple
entablatures, and with an upper feature similar in
style, but with Corinthian pilasters and broken pediments, and flanked by the customary pyramidal adornments.

10. A Doorway, Mexico City

9. House of Alvarado at Coyoacan

Wall treatment in all-over Patterns, Mexico City

THE Mudejar (Christianized Moorish) influence in ornament appeared so early in the life of the colony that one might say that it affected the very earliest manifestations of decoration, and, instead of disappearing with later developments, it persisted during the whole life of the Colony up to the *Academismo* itself at the very end of the Vice-Regal period. The traces of Mudejar influence, therefore, affected the character of practically all of the Colonial work.

This tendency made its earliest appearance in the decoration of walls with patterns made in lime mortar in geometric, or polygonal, forms, often highly Arabic in character, which covered the entire wall surface of certain buildings, recalling strongly the similar use of all-over ornament on the walls of many houses of Segovia, and the Cathedral of Saragossa in Old Spain.

The house in the Calle del Relox presents a beautiful example of this work in characteristic Arabic polygons, relieved by a charming border, while the walls of another house in the Calle 2 de Abril show a variant in the form of large panels, filled with a design of rather plain mouldings, whose volutes suggest an Aztec feeling, surrounded by a highly-decorated border. The whole effect here is Plateresque rather than Mudejar. Many other examples of this sort of decoration are found in and near the City of Mexico, including the churches of San Hipólito and San Juan de Dios, several old houses, and the upper part of the walls of the church of Tepozatlán.

[57]

11. WALL TREATMENTS IN ALL-OVER PATTERNS, MEXICO CITY

12. WALL TREATMENTS IN ALL-OVER PATTERNS, MEXICO CITY

PLATE 13

Corner of Palace of the Mayorazgo de Guerrero

THE great houses of the seventeenth and eighteenth centuries developed a unique type of façade in two stories. The plain surfaces of the walls were faced with crimson *tezontle,* a highly porous volcanic stone laid in blocks eight or ten inches square, sometimes in pattern, and closely fitted together without mortar. This surface of velvety texture was relieved by the trimmings of gray *chiluca,* often richly carved, which bordered the doors and windows. The fine tradition of Old Spain which concentrated the ornament about the portals, leaving the rest of the building comparatively plain, was followed, and the windows were simply treated by slightly arching the tops and carrying the architraves up to the cornice, forming a characteristic sort of transom panel over each window.

At the street corners a sort of turret was built, perhaps a reminiscence of the defensive bastion, of early Colonial days, and perhaps merely recalling the corner towers often seen in Spain. The angle of this turret was decorated with a richly treated niche, usually accommodating a statuette of religious nature.

Turrets, or battlements, on the tops of the houses were the prerogatives of important military officials, such as members of the Court of Audience, while other important persons were permitted to have breastworks, or parapets, formed of inverted arches between pilasters which were topped with pinnacles.

PLATE 14

Portal of the Palace of the Mayorazgo de Guerrero

THIS is one of the finest domestic doorways in the capital. The entrance is framed by two Ionic columns of perfect purity, which enclose a beautifully treated entrance way. The Baroque lintel is especially delightful. An iron balcony crowns the lower part and forms the base for a pair of Corinthian columns on pedestals, between which is a charming window in a frame of fretwork. The whole is topped by an elaborate carved motif, which contained the family arms before they were cut away.

The opposite corner is occupied by a similar house, built by the same family, which produces a magnificent effect of symmetry at the street corner.

13. Corner of Palace of the Mayorazgo de Guerrero

14. Portal of the Palace of the Mayorazgo de Guerrero

PLATE 15

Chapel of the Tercer Orden de San Francisco, Cuernavaca

THIS venerable church was built about 1529–30 at
the instance of Cortés. Its somewhat jumbled façades,
aged to a brilliant yellow, rise above the arid expanse
of the cathedral enclosure. The side portal, with its
half dome, is a striking feature, as is the bank of tombs
built beside it between the buttresses. The main front
is rudely carved, probably by Indian workmen, in
primitive fashion. The dome at the left, seen above
the pointed battlements of the enclosing wall, is that of
Nuestra Senora de Guadalupe, a later church which
adjoins the entrance to the Borda Gardens.

PLATE 16

View of La Parroquia, Taxco

THE massive bulk of the great church, with its fine
dome and towers, rises above the hilly streets of the
picturesque city. It would be hard to find a better
silhouette even in Europe. The façade of the church is
shown in Plate 77.

15. Chapel of the Tercer Orden de San Francisco,
Cuernavaca

16. View of La Parroquia, Taxco

PLATE 17

Under the Portales, Puebla

ONE of the " cool covered colonnades " of Mexico. These *Portales,* or arcaded sidewalks, so much admired in Europe and desired in America, are in Mexico a reality. Note the stone-flagged floor, the tasteful columns, and beamed ceiling. Nearer the center of the city the *Portales* are busy places — the abode of public typists, candy vendors, and much intriguing and exotic street life.

PLATE 18

Cathedral Cloister, Cuernavaca

CUERNAVACA CATHEDRAL was founded in 1529 by the Franciscans, and is a place of great interest. The cloisters betoken their age by the character of the columns and arches, delicious architectural combinations of old rose and honey color, stone built, gracious, massive, and eternal.

18. Cathedral Cloister, Cuernavaca

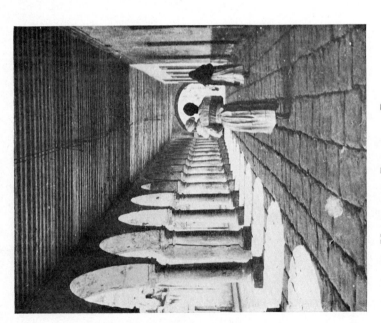

17. Under the Portales, Puebla

PLATE 19

Detail, House of Tiles

THIS plate shows highly interesting window trim
and pilasters in the lower story, as well as the pattern
of the tile panels in blue, white and yellow. The line
of the tile border seems to show Chinese influence of
some sort. Note the terminations at the bottoms of the
window architraves.

PLATE 20

Window, Las Vizcainas

THE Convent of Las Vizcainas (the Biscayans),
sometimes known as the Colegio de la Paz, is a vast
pile whose façades, 500 feet long, of red *tezontle*, have
suffered from settlement. Three rich Biscayan mer-
chants were walking home together one evening in the
year 1732, when they were struck by the poverty and
forsaken appearance of the young girls of the vicinity.
Upon learning that no schools existed in this quarter
of the city, they resolved to found a seminary into
which girls might be received and properly educated.
By 1767 the founders had expended $583,000, a great
sum for the time. The school is still continued, and is
said to be admirably managed.

The architecture, though peculiar, is distinctive.

20. Window, Las Vizcainas

19. Detail, "House of Tiles"

PLATE 21

Detail, Cloister of La Merced, Mexico City

THIS beautiful cloister, the most elaborate in the capital, is a splendid example of Plateresque work in Mexico and is unique of its kind in the Republic. The second story has two arches to one in the first, probably the only example of this type in Mexico, and the effect of the decoration recalls the most elaborate terra cotta work of North Italy. The detail of the decoration which covers the shafts of the columns is especially notice-able, as well as the diamond-like facets of the arches.

21. DETAIL, CLOISTER OF LA MERCED, MEXICO CITY

PLATE 22

Cloister of La Merced

THE site for a monastery of the Order of Mercy in this locality was granted on September 22, 1533, as there were few inhabitants in the vicinity and no religious establishment. The first small convent was not completed until 1593, but the order prospered and acquired additional land so that, in 1634, the first stone of the magnificent church was laid. The cloisters were finished in 1703.

PLATE 23

Upper Windows, La Concepcion, Mexico City

THESE are good examples of Mexican Renaissance in one of its best aspects. The proportions of the windows and their frames will repay study, as well as the very Spanish employment of cartouches between them.

The church was dedicated in 1665, but restored in 1809.

22. CLOISTER OF LA MERCED

23. UPPER WINDOWS, LA CONCEPCION, MEXICO CITY

PLATE 24

Doorway at Xochimilco

THIS well-designed old doorway is placed in the center of a great wall of stucco-covered masonry, unrelieved by any decoration except its color, a riot of old rose overlaying an undertone of lemon yellow.

PLATE 25

Façade, San Augustín Acolman

NEAR historic Texcoco the great bulk of this antique church rises above the *ameno valle,* as Villaseñor called it, a veritable stone fortress of the church, almost recalling the fortified convents of the Middle Ages. Its immense weight has proved too much for the yielding soil, so that it has sunk in the ground more than a meter, which injures the proportion of its main doorway.

The façade, of the purest and finest Renaissance type, is remarkable as being one of the few examples in Mexico which is apparently free from any local influence. The semi-circular arch, flanked by garlanded columns in the purest style of the Spanish Renaissance, the treatment of the statues on either side, and the ornaments and decoration of the frieze, all suggest the hand of a Spaniard unaffected by any Indian or other Colonial surroundings. High on the façade at the left of the window are the arms of Castile, Leon and Granada, balanced at the right by a local symbol.

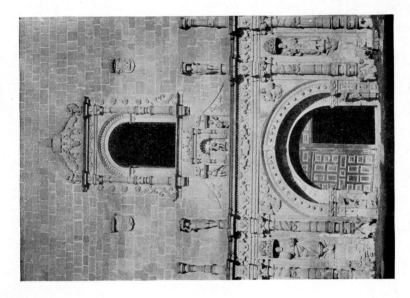

25. Façade, San Augustín Acolman

24. Doorway at Xochimilco

Details, San Augustín Acolman

THE similarity of these details to those of various Renaissance buildings of Old Spain, the Hospital de Santa Cruz at Toledo for example, has led to the theory that the work may come from the hand of the famous Enrique de Egas himself, if not that of Covarrubias or Berruguete. The interior archivolt is decorated with reliefs of cherubims alternating with fruits; the exterior with pears, apples, and pomegranates, and the intrados with all sorts of viands, fish, vegetables, and birds, on thirteen plates, probably an allusion to the Last Supper. An old inscription states that the work was finished in 1560, and another, high up in the interior, says in part, *Año de 1558 se Hiso*. Researches of recent date seem to prove, however, that the unknown designer of this beautiful work was not a Spaniard, but a provincial.[1]

The interior is remarkable for its frescoes, some of which, lately uncovered by cleaning the walls, prove to have been executed in the Roman manner at the time the church was built.

[1] *Arte Colonial*, by D. Manuel Romero de Terreros.

27. Details, San Augustín Acolman

26. Details, San Augustín Acolman

PLATE 28

The Cathedral of Mexico and the Sagrario

THESE splendid buildings, which are actually two separate churches, form together what is easily the finest ecclesiastical group in North America, and one of the finest in the world, while the cathedral's dimensions (387 feet long, 177 feet wide) give it rank among the world's largest churches. The main façade, shown in the plate, faces south on the Plaza de la Constitucion, the main square of the city, and the church occupies the site of the great *teocalli* of the city of Moctezuma.

The two splendid towers, built of warm yellow stone, rise to a height of 203 feet. It is interesting to note the almost exact similarity between the lower stories of these towers and the second story of the towers of the Escorial in Spain, the masterpiece of Herrara. The upper portions of the towers were not completed until after 1788, and are more interesting than their Spanish prototype. The bell-shaped domes which crown the towers rest on an octagonal base contained within a square pavilion, which is certainly a most successful solution of the problem of combining dignity and lightness in a Renaissance belfry.

The towers are occupied by a number of bells, of which the largest, *Santa Maria de Guadalupe*, is 16½ feet high, 10 feet wide at the base, and is said to weigh 13½ tons. It was cast in Tacubaya, a suburb, in 1792.

The façade is divided into three sections by two massive buttresses capped by great consols, and the three portals, which are treated with simple Doric orders, carry above them bas reliefs framed with twisted columns and elaborate cappings. The corner stone was laid in 1573, and final dedication occurred in 1667. An inscription over the entrance bears the date of 1672, but the upper portion of the façade was completed by Manuel Tolsa perhaps around 1804, and is in the best vein of the academic style prevalent at that time.

In plan the Cathedral of Mexico is a *Catedral-Salón* very similar to those built by Gil de Hontañon at Salamanca and Segovia, but the Gothic intention is not followed out in the interior which is strongly *herreriana* with its lofty fluted Doric piers and simple vaulting. Nevertheless it is a majestic and noble interior, even though it is marred by the location of the choir in the middle of the nave according to Spanish custom.

PLATE 29

Dome of the Cathedral of Mexico

THE dome of the cathedral was completed by addition of the slender lantern by Manuel Tolsa at the beginning of the nineteenth century. It is claimed that Tolsa purposely reduced the diameter of the lantern in order not to compete with the noble towers. The effect is unusual, but improves upon acquaintance. The balustrades of the roof and the bell-shaped domes of the main towers are also of Tolsa's design. (*See also* PLATE 56.)

28. THE CATHEDRAL OF MEXICO AND THE SAGRARIO

29. DOME OF THE CATHEDRAL OF MEXICO

PLATE 30

Interior of the Cathedral of Mexico

ALTHOUGH the architecture is severely Doric, the elaborate railings, altars, organ, etc., supply the necessary amount of richness to complete a highly sumptuous effect. The wood floor, while comfortable for worshippers, rather detracts from the general impression, but there are noble vistas, soaring heights, gorgeous pictures and picturesque corners, punctuated and relieved by the groups of black-clad worshippers, which make of the interior one of the great effects of the world's church architecture.

30. INTERIOR OF THE CATHEDRAL OF MEXICO

PLATE 31

Domes of El Carmen, San Angel

THE practice of encrusting or facing domes, towers, and walls with glazed tiles was very common in Mexico, and the number of buildings so decorated can be counted by hundreds, perhaps thousands. Among all these none are more charming than the three domes of the convent church of Nuestra Señora del Carmen at San Angel, dating from about 1628. The colors are principally blue, white, green and yellow. The designs are beautiful in themselves and are different for each dome. Some of the coats-of-arms are magnificent. The finials, glazed modeled figures, ornaments, etc., are also in glazed earthenware, as well as the little steps which are arranged to aid in ascending the outside of the domes to the lanterns. The effect of the group, seen in brilliant sunshine against the deep blue sky, is dazzling and brilliant. The domes can be closely examined from the flat roof of the church, which is frequently visited for the splendid view it affords of the Valley of Mexico, looking across the glossy foliage of the cool gardens close at hand to the snow-clad peaks of Popocatapetl and Iztaccihuatl.

PLATE 32

Convento del Carmen, San Angel

ONE of the domes referred to above is seen in this picture, as well as the bell tower. The rough and time-stained masonry of the exterior walls is of red and black stone, with the mortar brought well out and showing on the face. The convent contains many passages with rough plastered walls and floors of rough red tile, a library of priceless vellum-bound volumes in a fascinating tile-floored and rough-plastered chamber, and a sacristy and refectory containing much good tile work, as well as important paintings and ancient furniture. Under one of the chapels are buried forty-five American soldiers who served in the war of 1847–48.

The church and convent buildings form one of the most interesting and beautiful groups to be found in Mexico.

31. Domes of El Carmen, San Angel

32. Convento del Carmen, San Angel

PLATE 33

Church of San Domingo, Puebla

THE domed and tiled tower contrasting with the massive white buttresses of this church form a typical Mexican composition.

PLATE 34

Gateway, San Francisco Acatepec

THE old tiled church of San Francisco Acatepec lies a short distance from Cholula, whose decaying *teocallis* are conspicuous landmarks for miles around.

The capricious, yet well-proportioned, form of this gateway, with its arch and steps, is a typical Mexican treatment.

34. GATEWAY, SAN FRANCISCO ACATEPEC

33. CHURCH OF SAN DOMINGO, PUEBLA

PLATE 35

Rear of the Cathedral, Puebla

THE Cathedral of Puebla, the beautiful if somewhat severe sister of the metropolitan church of Mexico City, is assuredly one of the great churches of the world, and a masterpiece of its architect, Juan Gomez de Mora. Its noble façade and lofty twin towers dominate the lovely city of Puebla as cathedral towers should, but the most charming part of the exterior is the tumbled mass of chapels, domes and belfries at the rear, where a broad flight of steps leads up between great stone pillars to the rather weedy cathedral enclosure. This end of the church is built of a brilliantly warm yellow stone, which is joined at the end by a little rose-colored and white plastered house with lightly corbelled balconies of masonry, an outside stair, and windows grilled with heavy iron, a perfect composition for an operatic setting.

PLATE 36

A Patio at Puebla

EVEN in the humbler abodes the interiors of the houses are fascinating. The balconies which surround this simple courtyard are supported on corbels in the style of the locality.

The flower pots along the railing are an indication of the Mexican's universal love for beauty.

35. REAR OF THE CATHEDRAL, PUEBLA

36. A PATIO AT PUEBLA

PLATE 37

Haçienda Church Door

SOME one has estimated that Mexico has nine thousand churches of genuine architectural interest and only a short period of exploration is needed to convince one of the truth of such a statement.

This little church, built in a locality which to a stranger appears not to be a place at all, but just somewhere near San Juan Teotihuacan, is idiomatic, artistic, and altogether a cheerful object to meet in a dusty day's drive. The *peon* on the sun-baked pavement by the sagging door, the twisted columns, and the Aztec-like decoration of the bases, are all of the very essence of Mexico. Curiously enough, the interior of the church, carried out in gray stone, is of an irreproachable Doric chastity, which would almost be extreme in New England.

One cannot describe such work as the architecture of this doorway as Churrigueresque in the sense that the word is used in Spain. The fashion may have originally come from the mother country, but the Colonial architects and their Indian assistants developed from it a living style, indigenous to the soil, and Mexican to the core. The Chapel of the Well, the Sagrario, and this little church, are veritable jewels of a sparkling and spontaneous type of architecture which need fear no comparison with the leading European models of the period; and, best of all, it looks as if its designer and workmen alike had enjoyed every minute of the time they were engaged in its fabrication.

An interesting thought is suggested by the light that

is shed on the degree of civilization which produced
such sculptures as are found above this door on the
chapels of out-of-the-way villages and haçiendas,
when compared with the contemporary productions of
the English colonies.

37. Hacienda Church Door

PLATE 38

House at Taxco

THIS delightful little façade, with its all-over decorations in stucco and well-proportioned doorway and windows, is said to have been occupied by the explorer Humboldt during his famous visit to Mexico.

The clean streets of the town, paved in patterns and for centuries innocent of wheeled traffic, are shown in the picture, which also gives an idea of the character of the place, which was long famous for the riches of its mines and their lavish owner, José de la Borda.

PLATE 39

A Typical Pueblan House

PUEBLA, as the home and birthplace of enameled faience, quite properly contains many tiled houses, some of which are of great beauty. The walls above the stone base are often covered with unglazed red tiles, at the corners of which are inserted small square tiles glazed in blue, white, or other colors. The windows are furnished with iron balconies, and the stone architraves of the upper story are carried up to the cornice in the typical Mexican manner, forming panels above the windows. According to the custom of the plateau country the roof is flat and the cornice is given only slight projection. The lower windows are heavily barred.

39. A Typical Pueblan House

38. House at Taxco

PLATE 40

Tower of San Francisco, Puebla

PUEBLA is one of the handsomest cities in the Republic, well paved and clean in a manner unknown north of the Rio Grande. In the central parts its rectangularly laid out streets are full of churches, houses, and arcades of an architectural interest and refinement exceptional even for Mexico, but in the eastern quarter, across the little stream which divides the town into two unequal parts, there is a picturesque suburb which contains among its cubical white houses some important churches as well as entertaining vistas. The picture shows the tower of San Francisco, a morsel of the true *herreriana*, the white houses of the suburb, and the trees of the little Paseo which contains the statue of General Zaragoza, the young general who, at Puebla, on the *Cinco de Mayo*, 1862, drove a superior French army back to the coast. A grateful country founded its national holiday in memory of this feat.

PLATE 41

A Pulqueria

THE wine of the country in the plateau region is *pulque*, a fermented beverage made from the juice of the *maguey* plant, having about the same percentage of alcohol as beer, and tasting like a blend of cider and paregoric, which, incidentally, proves better than it sounds. Many of the shops which dispense this beverage are provided with façades highly decorated by native artists in brilliant colors. The paintings in this case represent scenes from a bull fight, and recall the frescoes of ancient Pompeii.

40. Tower of San Francisco, Puebla

41. A Pulqueria

PLATE 42

A Street at Puebla

IRON-BARRED windows, white towers, deep shadows, and a brilliantly blue sky make this typical Mexican composition, ready for the water-colorist's brush. The photographs cannot reproduce the delicate, reflected lights of the white wall at the left.

PLATE 43

Church and Atrium, Puebla

A FORE court, or atrium, lends dignity to any church, and this well-proportioned gateway, backed by cypresses, is an appropriate introduction to the beautiful baroque church behind it. The shapes of the windows over the entrances of churches are of ever-recurring interest.

43. CHURCH AND ATRIUM, PUEBLA

42. A STREET AT PUEBLA

The Casa de Alfeñique, Puebla

A FORM of Churrigueresque, or, perhaps more properly, the neo-Plateresque, is the splendid Casa de Alfeñique which is carried out in the idiomatic manner common in Puebla. The exterior walls are faced with dull red tiles carrying glazed colored tiles set in at the corners, while the trimmings are of white stone. The elegantly thin balconies, elaborately carved cornices, and the special feature of a whimsical corner balcony at the third story, protected by a light stone canopy, are all features of this Pueblan manner. The panels above the windows are preserved, and the belt course executes a delightful double-shuffle over the main entrance. The name *alfeñique* means almond cake, or gingerbread, an allusion to the lightness and capriciousness of the decoration. The interior patio is small, but contains a beautiful carved stairway and good iron work, very hard to photograph on account of the restricted space.

Puebla, on the main road from the capital to Vera Cruz, was in contact with all the traffic to and from Seville, the headquarters of the Convent of the Indies, and must have felt the Arabic or Mudejar influence very strongly. The city contains quite a number of houses of this type, located generally at street corners, and furnished with corner balconies and projecting canopies. Frequently the trim of the windows is given an even greater allowance of ornament.

44. THE CASA DE ALFEÑIQUE, PUEBLA

45. THE CASA DE ALFEÑIQUE, PUEBLA

PLATE 46

Convent of Santa Maria de los Angeles at Churubusco

THE Convent Church at Churubusco, which was built about 1678, contains the pretty little tiled chapel of San Antonio Abad nestling in an angle at the base of the massive tower. The chapel with its diminutive dome is entirely covered with glazed and colored tiles. Beside it is a simple and well-proportioned arched doorway with niche and pediment above, in the earlier manner. The convent itself has great historical interest, as it formed the support of the right of the Mexican line at the battle of Churubusco, August 20, 1847. The defenders, under Generals Rincon and Anaya, put up a stubborn resistance against the heavier artillery of the Americans, and only surrendered when their ammunition was exhausted. The walls and tower of the convent have aged to a delicate rose color, shading into a delicious yellow. The church contains some beautiful tile work, and other interesting carvings and paintings; and the locality, now a region of peaceful maize fields, is one of the most interesting in the Valley.

46. Convent of Santa Maria de los Angeles at Churubusco

PLATE 47

Capilla del Pocito, Guadalupe Hidalgo

THE most important example of the combination of Plateresque and Mudejar influences upon the baroque style of the Vice-Regal period is that true jewel of Colonial architecture, called the "Chapel of the Well," at Villa de Guadalupe, or Guadalupe Hidalgo, three miles from Mexico City, and one of the most important pilgrimage towns in the world, which was made famous by the apparition of the Blessed Virgin on December 9, 1531. In connection with that apparition a healing spring gushed forth from a barren hillside, and it was over this spring that this chapel was built, in 1777–91, by the architect, Don Francisco Guerrero Torres.

The form of the building is not only beautiful but highly original and appropriate to its purpose. The plan is formed by the principal chapel, which is elliptical, and by the small, circular chapel annexed to it which covers the sacred well. In addition there is a small sacristy at the rear. The building is about 55 feet wide by 95 feet in extreme depth.

The plan is expressed exactly by the exterior. The smaller circular chapel in front is about 20 feet in diameter, and contains the legendary well, a somewhat sulphurous bubbling spring within a curb some six feet across, provided with a copper pail which is constantly in use by devout pilgrims.

Both domes as well as the capriciously modeled upper portions of the walls are covered with blue and

[137]

white *azulejos* alternated in chevron-like formation with rib lines of yellow and crowned by lanterns of similar shape, also in tiles and finished with a cross.

The effect of this beautiful building is due not only to its original and beautiful design, but to the use of polychromy, and to the contrast of the dazzling blue and white of the domes with the dark purplish-red of the walls. From any point of view this little known chapel must eventually take its place among the finest architectural gems of the Renaissance as a building original, idiomatic, absolutely suited to its purpose, and frankly indigenous to its native soil.

From the preliminary chamber access is had to the larger chapel, which is utilized for religious services and contains four altars, commemorating the four appearances of the Virgin of Guadalupe. There are two lateral doors, and a door to the sacristy opposite to that from the Pocito.

The façades of both chapels are curved in plan, built of red *tezontle* with trimmings of lighter stone, and provided with windows in the symbolical form of a star.

The smaller chapel is roofed by a spherical, and the larger by an elliptical, dome.

PLATE 48

Church Door, Villa de Guadalupe

Santa Coleta, just east of the Basilica of Guadalupe, was built about 1782–87. The recessed central part of the entrance with its ample pediment has a fine swing of noble proportions. The square in front is crowded with vendors of candles and objects of piety.

[138]

48. Church Door, Villa de Guadalupe

47. Capilla del Pocito, Guadalupe Hidalgo

PLATE 49

Main Door, Capilla del Pocito

THE principal doorway is curved in plan, following the interior, and is decorated in the first story with two pairs of Corinthian columns, one pair on each side of the door with niches, and above two other pairs of columns, likewise Corinthian, but more highly ornamented. The base is also of light stone, and the niches are backed with tiles.

PLATE 50

Side Door, Capilla del Pocito

THE side door is also on a curved plan, and is given a whimsical form of the Doric order, with an easily flowing sort of pediment and a brilliant star window above. Note the undulating lines of the pilasters and lintel, and the delightful fretwork borders of the *tezontle* wall panels.

This plate also shows the tile pattern and one of the elaborate dormers.

50. Side Door, Capilla del Pocito

49. Main Door, Capilla del Pocito

PLATE 51

A Chapel at Guadalupe Hidalgo

THIS busy little city, the site of the famous shrine
of Our Lady of Guadalupe, although overrun by pilgrims (200,000 reported in one day in 1926), possesses
a few cool and shady corners, of which this is one. The
little parks, or *alamedas,* are one of the joys of Mexican travel. Almost every town has one, always kept
clean, shady, and provided with an iron band stand.
The traveller would be grateful if more of them were
provided with seats.

PLATE 52

A Mexican Alameda

A SCENE combining several characteristic features:
the church with its dome, the shady little park, the
cobbly street, and the omnipresent Indian vendor of
eatables, with her three-legged umbrella and not much
else. Her stock consists of a handful of peanuts, two
or three tomatoes, some *tunas* or prickly pear fruit,
and maybe a few other strange but highly colored vegetables. She sits there all day and no one ever saw her
make a sale, but, on the other hand, her overhead is
small, and her stock in case of necessity can always
be eaten.

52. A Mexican Alameda

51. A Chapel, Guadalupe Hidalgo

PLATE 53

Detail, Capilla del Pocito

THE carving of this building repays careful study, for its richness, balance, and originality. The central window above the door is star shaped and contains a little figure of the Virgin. All around the window is a mass of the richest sculpture, resembling chased silver and composed chiefly of the forms of little angels. This freedom from the confining forms of European precedent is a fascinating feature of Mexican work, which indicates artistically a far greater independence of the mother country than was the case in the English colonies.

PLATE 54

Fountain in Patio of the "House of Tiles"

THE interior of the Casa de los Azulejos is a worthy adjunct to the exterior. There is a noble patio, surrounded by slender columns of graceful but unusual design, and containing a baroque fountain of gray stone recalling properties of both the baroque and Mudejar styles.

A grand stone staircase, wainscoted with tiles of Chinese appearance, leads to the main floor which contains an elaborate chapel.

All the details of this building are surprisingly original and beautiful. The graceful stone columns of the patio are particularly pleasing. The patio is now utilized as a restaurant.

53. Detail, Capilla del Pocito

54. Fountain in Patio of the "House of Tiles"

PLATE 55

Details from the "House of Tiles" in Mexico City

THE very finest example of the Baroque-Plateresque style applied to domestic work is the incomparable house of the Conde del Valle de Orizaba, better known as the Casa de los Azulejos, or House of Tiles, which was, if not the most sumptuous or rich, still the most beautiful residence in the colony. Its façade not only presents much rich carving of Plateresque character in its pilasters, copings, and around its windows and doors, but the entire area of its external walls is covered with blue, white, and yellow Puebla glazed tiles. The rather oriental character of the designs has led to the belief that the tiles were imported from China, but Edwin Atlee Barber in his book, *The Maiolica of Mexico,* states unhesitatingly that they are the usual tin-enameled pottery such as was produced at Puebla about the middle of the eighteenth century. Most of the tiles are slightly curved, probably having been warped in burning, which produces a not unpleasing wall texture.

The history of the house is unusual. The original structure, built perhaps around 1596, was acquired by the spendthrift son of one of the Condes del Valle de Orizaba, to whom he had been the cause of frequent sorrow and chagrin. On one occasion the old Count, convinced that his son would squander his entire patrimony, exclaimed, employing a phrase then used in connection with a spendthrift in Mexico:

"You will never build a house of tiles, my son."

As a matter of fact, the youth mended his ways and actually built the beautiful house, a reproduction of which we see here. The mansion has had a varied history. Under President Diaz it was occupied by the aristocratic Jockey Club. During a later period it was put to a popular use, but has since been purchased by Mr. Sanborn, an American, who utilizes it for business purposes, while carefully conserving its architectural character.

55. DETAIL FROM THE "HOUSE OF TILES" IN MEXICO CITY

PLATE 56

Cathedral Tower, Mexico City

THE design of the belfry stories of the two great
towers is a happy solution of this problem which occurs
in many Renaissance churches. To combine massiveness and lightness is always difficult. In this case the
square exterior pavilion encloses an octagonal inner
structure which contains the bells, and by its shape
and mass provides the requisite effect of solidity with
play of light and shade. The bell-like tops which form
such a distinctive feature belong to the later academic
period.

PLATE 57

Façade of the Sagrario, Mexico City

THIS church, which adjoins the Cathedral, is perhaps, all in all, the finest Churrigueresque development of church architecture in Mexico, and ranks with La Santísima and the church at Tepozatlán as one of the finest flowers of the Colonial period at its climax in the eighteenth century. The architect was the talented Lorenzo Rodríguez, likewise the designer of La Santísimà. Adjoining the Cathedral of Mexico on the east, of which it seems to be a part, it succeeds marvellously in forming a harmonious composition seen from any point of view. The façades are of the usual red *tezontle* relieved with light stone trimmings, and the two highly original fronts of the nave and transept form one of the most striking features of the great square of the city.

It is difficult to describe the intricate design of these two fronts, and yet the ensemble is perfectly simple and effective. The great Spanish lesson of contrasting a field of intensely rich carving against an absolutely plain background, so little understood in English-speaking countries, was never better exemplified than in this beautiful Mexican church.

57. Façade of the Sagrario, Mexico City

56. Cathedral Tower, Mexico City

PLATE 58

Details of the Sagrario

THE door motifs of course first challenge our interest. There is frankly no attempt to adapt ornament to construction, but it seems as if the architect, out of pure joy in his work, had developed the design of his fancy and applied it against the wall of the church, just as one of the great carved and gilded retablos is planted against the interior wall of a chapel, and the idea is justified by the resulting effect.

The plans, which provided for a building raised upon a Greek cross, a thing unusual in itself in Mexico, were completed in 1749. The triangular façades and the rather low and flattish dome seem to imply an effort to subordinate the mass to that of the cathedral adjoining. One must rejoice that this lovely addition to the cathedral group came into being at the full flowering epoch of the capital's artistic life, and before the icy current of the *Academismo* had checked the generous flow of native genius. Correctly classic chapels exist everywhere, but only Mexico could have produced the Sagrario. As Barroso well says, it is worthy of admiration, study, and respect.

58. Details of the Sagrario

PLATE 59

Basilica of Guadalupe

THIS splendid church, which contains the *tilma* of the *peon* Juan Diego bearing the miraculous portrait of the Virgin, was completed in 1709 at enormous cost.

The entrance motif is well-proportioned and well-detailed, of light stone against a background of red *tezontle*.

The interior of the church is dignified, well-proportioned, and attractive. The silver railings of the chancel and galleries are the marvel of many visitors.

PLATE 60

La Santísima Trinidad, Mexico City

THIS church, which has, next to the Sagrario Metropolitano (plates 27, 57, 58), the most important and elaborate Churrigueresque façade in the City of Mexico, was designed by Lorenzo Rodríguez and was dedicated January 17, 1783.

The plan of the church, which is backed against buildings on two sides, is a Latin cross. A dome covers the junction of the nave and transept, and a single tower rises at the corner.

The entrance is decorated with a magnificent motif in three stories, framed by elaborately rusticated border pilasters, or buttresses. The main door, beautifully paneled, carries above it a shield with the papal insignia, and on each side two pilasters formed of inverted pyramids with sculptures of popes between. A great relief of the Holy Trinity occupies the center of the second story, flanked on either side by pilasters similar to those below, and more papal sculptures between. The third story is narrower, and is composed mainly of a great window with curvilinear lines, framed in a sort of pylon, and flanked by carved pinnacles.

The general proportions are good, but are somewhat marred by the sinking of the entire fabric in the yielding sub-soil. The interruption of the cornices of the first and second stories by the central feature of the façade also tends to break up the harmony of the composition.

The church possesses a lateral entrance of great harmony and beauty as well.

60. La Santísima Trinidad, Mexico City

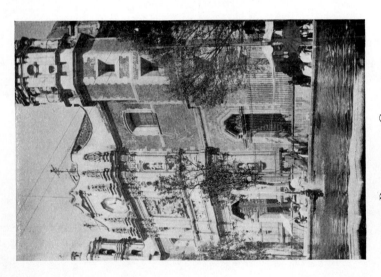

59. Basilica of Guadalupe

PLATE 61

Dome and Tower of La Santísima

THE dome springs from an octagonal drum which has a window in each side, decorated with carvings in stone. The sections of the dome are covered with *azulejos*, a Mudejar detail worth noticing in a church of this type. A lantern of the usual type crowns the whole.

The tower rises from the ground, the plain walls of red *tezontle* with rusticated corners forming a background to the fretwork of the main façade. Beginning at the roof level it presents a rich belfry story corresponding to the main façade, but with twelve pilasters which are ingeniously arranged with three at each angle, so that one sees a pair on each side of the belfry arch on each of the four sides. The tower is terminated by a sort of dome in the form of the papal tiara, surmounted by a cross.

PLATE 62

Tower and Side Buttresses of La Santísima

A MOST effective view of this striking church is had from the side street towards the rear, where the mighty buttresses are seen to their best advantage.

Taken as a whole, this church possesses great unity, a quality sometimes lacking in the Baroque Colonial work. The relation between the two façades is good, and the entire mass, tower and dome, are in keeping with each other. La Santísima, with the Sagrario and the façade of Tepozatlán, form the most important group in this style.

61. Dome and Tower of La Santísima

62. Tower and Side Buttresses
of La Santísima

Plate 63

Tiled Seat and Fountain

THERE was no limit to the uses which were found
for the tin-enameled tiles of Puebla. Fountains, basins,
seats, and shrines were some of the garden accessories
which employed them.

This seat is in the beautiful garden of the government tobacco factory in Puente de Alvarado, Mexico
City, a palace designed by Tolsa and successively the
residence of the Condesa de Pérez Gálvez, Prince de
Iturbide, General Santa Anna, and the French Mar-
shal, Bazaine.

Plate 64

Gateway at Orizaba

ANOTHER example of Mexican garden work, always
fascinating and attractive.

[173]

63. TILED SEAT AND FOUNTAIN

64. GATEWAY AT ORIZABA

PLATE 65

House of the Masks, Mexico City

THE house now standing in the ancient Tlacópan Causeway, now Calle de la Ribera de San Cosme, in Mexico City, is one of the best examples of Churrigueresque art applied to domestic use. The house has only one story, and its façade presents three windows on each side of the central door. The central motif containing the door is unfinished. A system of rusticated blocks covers the entire surface. Between the windows, which are highly ornamented, there is an elaborate pilaster supporting a sort of caryatid, above which are richly decorated gargoyles that give the house the name of *Las Mascarones*, or House of the Masks. This highly original dwelling was begun by Don José de Mendoza, Conde del Valle de Orizaba. He died in 1771, before the exterior was completed. At that time he had spent $100,000 upon the house, a vast sum in those days of cheap labor. It was sold at auction in 1824, and made habitable.

The carving under the window sills is noteworthy, and typical in general design of much Mexican work.

PLATE 66

Cathedral and City Hall, San Luis Potosí

THE Baroque cathedral with its twisted columns and numerous niches was dedicated in 1737, and is flanked by the simple and dignified *Ayuntamiento*, or City Hall, with its cool loggias and massive piers. The clean but narrow street separates them from the Alameda, with its broad surrounding walk paved in neat squares of black and white stone, the evening promenade of the citizens, and the out-of-door *salón* of the city.

65. House of the Masks, Mexico City

66. Cathedral and City Hall, San Luis Potosí

PLATE 67

In the Borda Garden

THESE gardens were created by the same José de la Borda who caused the erection of the famous church of Taxco. The beautiful city of Cuernavaca, half way from the mines of Taxco to the capital, appealed to him as a sort of *Buen Retiro,* a place where he might satisfy his *penchant* for horticulture.

The garden, whose water channels and basins are now dry, must have, in its day, recalled those of El Generalife at Granada with their aqueducts, fountains, great glassy pools of water, and magnificent trees.

Even now the flora of the garden possesses much interest, while the views from it are superb. The garden adjoins the famous *barranca,* across which the soldiers of Cortés swarmed on a fallen tree to capture the ancient Aztec stronghold.

67. IN THE BORDA GARDEN

PLATE 68

Panelled Doors

FROM a private collection. The intricate panelling suggests the Arabic work of Old Spain.

PLATE 69

An Old Door

FROM the Capilla de Soledad, adjoining the Sagrario. Here the type of panelling follows the flowing and undulating lines of the building itself.

68. Panelled Doors

69. An Old Door

PLATE 70

Gilded Carving, Puebla

AN example of the wood carver's skill, of which hundreds of examples exist in altars, *sedilias*, and portals, all over the Republic.

PLATE 71

A Tiled Wall

A DETAIL of a Pueblan wall pattern, with a glazed tile insert and pictorial motif. The dark squares are unglazed red tiles, but all the rest is glazed. Entire buildings decorated in this manner are very common in Puebla, in fact are almost typical of the city.

71. A Tiled Wall

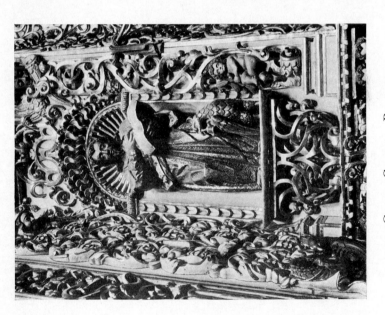

70. Gilded Carving, Puebla

PLATE 72
Church at Tepozatlán

THE third great example of the neo-Plateresque is the façade of the convent church of Tepozatlán. The church itself is of earlier construction, and the dome was influenced by other tendencies, but the façade, of clean cut stone, with its tower in two great stories, is magnificent. The *portada*, or great central motif, is flanked on each side by comparatively plain surfaces which give full relief to the brilliant play of light and shade in the carving. The ornament is of the finest cutting throughout, and the firm lines of the lower cornice, the slightly broken lines of the second, and the undulating profile of the cornice, which rises in successive elevations like the jets of a living fountain, combine to make it a masterpiece of its period. Statistics are a poor indication of artistic merit, but the richness of the façade may be judged by the fact that the tower and *portada* together contain 56 figures of angels, 118 heads of cherubims, and 146 figures of saints, a total of 320 figures, a veritable litany in stone, which almost recalls the glories of the Gothic cathedrals. The general layout is similar to others of the same style, viz. an arrangement of decorated pilasters enclosing niches and medallions in two stories, with an attic story, or *remate,* glorifying the whole. The tower also retains the characteristic arrangement of the corner pilasters, which results in showing two pilasters at each corner of each side.

The photograph also shows the surrounding wall with inverted circular capping, a sign of ecclesiastical authority.

[193]

The façade and tower may be qualified simply as magnificent, for they combine unity, not only in the character of their carving, but in the manner in which they are bound together by strong horizontal bands, strength in the solidity and simplicity of the *cubo* or base of the tower and flanking walls, and excellent proportion in the entire composition.

72. CHURCH AT TEPOZATLÁN

Interior of the Church at Tepozatlán

THE interior decoration of these temples was influenced by the Plateresque, which in its turn was strongly affected by the Gothic. In the case of Tepozatlán the heavily gilded retablos harmonize with the richness of the exterior, completing the unity of the whole scheme.

73, 74. Interior of the Church at Tepozatlán

PLATE 75

Detail of Portal, Tepozatlán

AN examination of the detail of this work reveals a crispness and lightness of touch easily comparable to the best early Spanish Renaissance; in fact, so brilliant and sparkling is the carving that one hesitates to believe that it is a work of the later period at all.

75. Detail of Portal at Tepozatlán

PLATE 76

The Noche Triste Memorial, Mexico City

THIS quaint monument in the Calle del Puente de Alvarado forms a corner of the enclosing wall of the Church of San Hipólito, and marks the spot where, on the terrible night of July 1, 1520, over 600 Spaniards were slain on the causeway which then connected the Aztec city of Tenochtitlán with the mainland, during their attempted retreat from the city.

The device represents a terrified Indian clasped in the embrace of an eagle, and recalls the tradition of an Indian who was selected by the gods to advise the Emperor Moctezuma of the danger which threatened him unless he forsook the sort of life he was leading.

PLATE 77

The "*Parroquia*" of Taxco

THE millionaire mining magnate, José de la Borda, who also created the famous Borda gardens at Cuernavaca, erected this church about 1757 as a token of gratitude for the good fortune which attended his mining ventures.

No expense was spared to make the building a perfect example of ecclesiastical design, and it is regarded as one of the most important churches, architecturally, in Mexico. The design suffers from the contraction of the bases, or *cubos*, of the towers, a defect which also appears in the church at Ocotlán, and which detracts from the usual massiveness of Spanish design. The intent may have been to increase the apparent height.

The dome, covered with glazed tiles in blue, orange, green, and white, carries at its base the words *Gloria á Dios en las alturas*, "Glory to God on the heights," a fitting Spanish paraphrase.

(*See also* PLATES *16* and *78*.)

76. THE NOCHE TRISTE MEMORIAL,
MEXICO CITY

77. THE "PARROQUIA" OF TAXCO

PLATE 78

A Window at Taxco

A DETAIL from La Parroquia.

PLATE 79

An Old Stone Escutcheon

MANY of the coats-of-arms which ornamented the façades of the ancient Spanish palaces were ordered removed by the Government of the Republic. Some were saved, and are contained in the National Museum.

79. An Old Stone Escutcheon

78. A Window at Taxco

PLATE 80

Pool in the Borda Garden, Cuernavaca

THIS delightful pool has a sentimental interest as
having been a favorite resort of the Empress Carlotta
during her unhappy reign. The bathing pavilions and
stone seats were then gay with the followers of the
brilliant court. This pool, or rather lake, for it is 40
feet wide and 500 feet long, forms the central or main
feature of the garden. (*See also* PLATE 67.)

PLATE 81

Old House, San Angel

A QUITE complete example of an old-time suburban
house, aristocratic evidently, by the scalloped parapets, or *almenas,* which could only betoken the abode
of a person of rank. The barred windows giving on the
street, and the enclosed garden, with the enormous
mass of crimson-purple bougainvillea contrasting with
the white walls, complete a most effective composition.

80. Pool in the Borda Garden, Cuernavaca

81. Old House, San Angel

PLATE 82

Palacio de Mineria, Mexico City

THE School of Mines, a vast, gloomy affair regarded as the masterpiece of the architect, Manuel Tolsa, was built in the years from 1797 to 1813, and is said to have cost at that time $1,500,000. The dimensions are inspiring, for the main façade has a length of 312 feet, and the principal *patio* is 86 feet square. Its mass and details are drawn from European sources and are correct and in good taste, but its effect is cold and formal in comparison with the productions of native taste in the structures built in preceding years. The patio and staircase, however, possess great majesty and need not fear comparison with the best European work of the period.

It is related that Tolsa was given only two months to make the plans for this enormous building, which may be an excuse for the serious settlements which mar the façade, amounting to at least three or four feet. The settlements began the year the building was finished, and have continued more or less ever since, although great sums have been expended in efforts to prevent it.

During his visit to Mexico in 1880, General Grant was lodged in this building.

PLATE 83

Stairway in Palacio de Mineria

THE treatment of the basement and *entresol* is worthy of note, as well as the two side porticoes, whose bases have sunk in the earth. The *patio* is probably the most interesting part of the building, and the stately stairway with the wide and easy steps and handsome balustrade should be better known.

82. Palacio de Mineria, Mexico City

83. Stairway in Palacio de Mineria

PLATE 84

The Church of El Carmen, Celaya

THIS church was the masterpiece of the architect, Francisco Eduardo Tresguerras, a real genius of the Renaissance, whose biography, had he lived in Italy, might have adorned the pages of another Vasari. He was born in Celaya in 1745, and the story of his life refutes the proverb about prophets being without honor in their own country, for it was his home town which gave him the opportunity to do his greatest work, the beautiful Church of El Carmen, which was dedicated in 1807 and cost $225,000, according to Terreros. He was compensated for his work during the years from 1802 to 1807 by an honorarium of 2000 *pesos* annually, which he took in real estate consisting of some small houses which existed until recently.

His own description of the church says that the dome is of the same height as the tower, 70 *varas* (195 feet), and is elliptical in plan, with eight windows in the drum, separated by pairs of Corinthian columns which, he says, give 90 square *varas* of light in the interior.

The dome, as well as the bell-like termination of the tower, are covered with *azulejos*, an interesting circumstance which shows the persistence of this practice up to the very end of the Vice-Regal period.

Tresguerras had the faculty of imparting a sort of graciousness to the details of his work which relieved it of the formality which characterized that of Tolsa. Terreros regards him as the greatest architect Mexico ever produced.

84. THE CHURCH OF EL CARMEN, CELAYA

Date Due

Date Due			
FEB 2 '44			
MAR 3 '47			
MAR 21 '47			
MAY 6 '59			